Komodo Dra

Trace Taylor

Some   ere in Asia
there are dragons…

Komodo dragons can grow to be 10 feet long. That's nearly the length of a small car.

See the **dragon**.

Komodos can easily spot nearby animals that are moving around, but may not be able to notice animals that are standing still.

2

See the **eye**.

Komodo noses cannot smell very well. Like a snake, the dragon uses its tongue to detect odors.

See the **nose**.

3

Using its forked tongue, the Komodo can smell its food up to 4 miles away.

See the **tongue**.

Komodos have about 60 teeth. Their teeth are covered by gum tissue. Every time they eat, they cut their own gums.

See the **mouth**.

5

Komodo dragons drool a lot. This drool is full of deadly bacteria and blood from their mouths.

See the **spit**.

The dragon's jaw is flexible and can open very wide. This allows the Komodo to swallow huge hunks of meat without choking.

See the **head**.

7

Komodo skin is made up of hard scales that protect them like a suit of armor. A thick suit of armor makes it difficult to feel things, but not for the Komodo. Each of its scales has 1 or more spots on it that are sensitive when touched.

See the **skin**.

Komodos can run faster than most humans. They can run up to 12 miles per hour, but only for short distances before they get too hot.

See the **legs**.

9

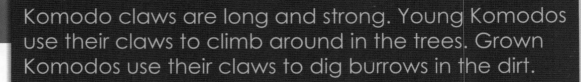

Komodo claws are long and strong. Young Komodos use their claws to climb around in the trees. Grown Komodos use their claws to dig burrows in the dirt.

See the **claws**.

When male Komodos fight for a female's attention, they use their tails to support themselves as they wrestle upright and try to throw each other to the ground.

See the **tail**.

Power Words

See

see

the

More About the Komodo...

13

ASIA

14

Komodo Island

Geographic Location

Islands are pieces of land surrounded by water. Komodo dragons live on 5 islands in Indonesia. These volcanic islands are dry and hot, with few plants or other vegetation. Three of these islands, including Komodo Island, are part of Komodo National Park, a protected habitat of the Komodo dragon.

15

Size Chart

3-foot long dog

6-foot tall person

10-foot long dragon

13-foot long car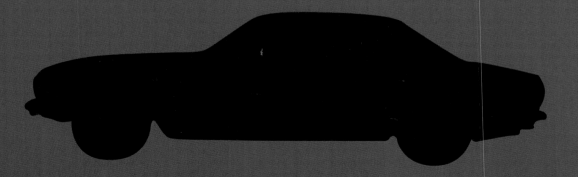

16

Fight for Survival

Newly hatched Komodos hide in the trees because any dragon that is bigger than they are will eat them, including their mom or dad. Even adult dragons will eat each other if they can. It's hard to be a Komodo dragon. Every day is a fight for survival.

Prey: Wild Boars

Wild boars are tough little pigs. They exist in many countries, but only in Indonesia will they come face to face with Komodo dragons. When they do, they had better watch out because dragons eat these little pigs.

Prey: Water Buffalo

Water buffalo might be big and tough, but they are no match for Komodo dragons. These buffalo often escape the dragon's grasp with only a bite or two, but even a single bite from the Komodo can be fatal.

Prey: Long-tailed Macaques

Long-tailed macaques live in the trees on the islands where Komodo dragons live. Even in the trees they are hunted by 3-foot long young, and hungry Komodos.

Coaching Tips for Parents and Teachers

Kids love to read READLINGS to parents and teachers because they CAN. Try these helpful tips.

Adults

- Read the book title and the first few pages to your child.

- Model using your finger to keep track of where you are.

- When your child can't figure out the picture, have him/her use the first letter sound as a clue.

- Remember that reading is problem solving. Help your child use all available clues.

Ready-to-Read Child

- Uses the patterns and pictures to read the rest of the book.

- Points to each word as he/she reads it.

- Uses the first letter sound to help with tricky pictures.

- Has FUN!

Can you match the words with the pictures?

tail

tongue

mouth

claws